Aunt Crystal & The Adverb Elevator

Sandy Ryerse

~ For my Dad ~

My very own Norman the Doorman!

I am so very thankful for the myriads of opportunities that you and Mom always encouraged me to take … and the example of selflessness and a giving heart.

Love, Sandy

ISBN 978-1-7387595-1-4

Aunt Crystal Press

www.sandyryerse.com

Cover design by GetCovers.com

How to Read this book . . .

You will find three symbols throughout the book (please notice that the symbols only happen when the person speaking is IN the elevator).

When you see this symbol 🔔 let a DING chime in your ears!

When you see this symbol 〰 let a RUMBLE roll through your whole body!

And when you see this symbol 💥 look up to your right and watch for a FLASH of light!

MONDAY

I SLUMPED DOWN IN the front seat, put on my grouchiest face, and slammed the car door. I could have stayed at Deshaun's house. His mother wouldn't have noticed one more kid. Besides, Deshaun, Chad, and Eric already had our week planned: ice hockey, floor hockey, ball hockey, road hockey, a little broom ball thrown in, and then of course more ice hockey. It would have been the perfect Spring Break with my three best friends.

Aunt Crystal's lime green car chugged along the highway like a Lego cart built by a three-year-old. I half expected the back tires to fall off and roll on by as Peterbilts and Freightliners plowed by us and shook us like we were a pair of dice in my old game of Trouble. I figured Aunt Crystal, my dad's only sister would bombard me with her old lady ideas of fun this week: Parcheesi, baking, watching game shows, and knitting while my parents took my little sister, Taryn, to a cheer competition in Syracuse, NY. I loved Aunt Crystal and all, but six days cooped up in an old apartment building—whoops, condo complex—with a boring old honeybee professor? Worst Spring Break ever.

A-hunka-hunka-hunka. A-hunka-hunka-hunka, sputter, sputter, hissssss. Aunt Crystal's prehistoric Beetle stalled as we stopped in the underground parking garage. I flung my ten-ton camo duffle bag over my shoulder as I forced open the door.

"Whoa." I jumped out and made sure that I didn't hit the sleek black convertible parked next to us. I took a quick picture with the cell phone Dad gave me for the week. That car had to be worth five hundred thousand buckaroonos. What kind of place did Aunt Crystal live in? Maybe pro hockey players or movie stars or trillionaires lived here.

"That Ferrari belongs to Truman Castle, the professional gamer." Aunt Crystal snickered at my gasp. Then she pointed to the yellow Bugatti decked out with tons of chrome that had just parked way down on the opposite side of the garage. "And that one belongs to the woman living in the penthouse, but I haven't met her yet."

A chauffeur, all dressed in black, helped a girl wearing a puffy robin-egg blue parka out of the passenger side. Was that Awish from my school? My stomach squeezed like a fist. Then the driver removed what looked like an aquarium from the trunk before he, and parka girl, walked toward a private elevator.

"Wowza! Penthouse? Is she a brain surgeon or something?" I stooped to admire my fresh flat-top haircut in the chrome mirror of the Ferrari and snapped a quick selfie.

"Something that pays a lot better than a university honeybee professor." Aunt Crystal snort-giggled and directed me to a doorway.

"This is awesome! This is what you need." I dragged my fingers carefully across the hood of a wild, neon-orange two-seater machine as we walked toward the entrance to the lobby. "Is this a motorcycle, or a car?" I took another selfie.

"That is called a Trike-bike. Technically, it's a motorcycle because you need a motorcycle license to drive it." My aunt wobbled on one leg with one knee propped up for balance. Juggling a few grocery bags, she searched for her key elbow-deep in her ginormous purse. Rinky-Dink cookies, cheesy crinkled chips, and a bunch of asparagus fell out of one bag onto the ground. "Oh fuzzy petunias," she murmured as her clunky curls bounced in front of her eyes.

Still intrigued by the motorcycle, I caught up to Aunt Crystal, picked up the broken cookies, and grabbed two bags from her arms. "It looks like something right out of the comic books." I nodded back at the Trike-bike.

At least when I got bored this week, I could slip down to the parking garage to check out the hardware. Just wait till the guys heard about this.

"And you think I would look good driving a trike-bike? Hmmmm. What are you saying?" She lifted a gold metal case high in her right hand. "Found it."

"I'm saying that I would go for millions of rides with you if you had one of those."

"And what about millions of rides in my wonderful Beetle?"

I didn't dare answer that one.

Aunt Crystal held the gold case against a silver plate on the wall to the right of the humongous black metal door to her building. It felt like we were going to walk into a bank vault. Clank. The powerful door unlocked and slid open slowly and pretty smoothly for its weight. It had to be ten tons.

"Double whoa."

The automatic door opened into the lobby of the condo. "Triple whoa." It sure didn't look like an apartment building to me. It felt like some futuristic planet with its bright lights and zippy music. Tap, tap, tap, tap, tap, tap. I took at least ten pictures as I stepped through the door.

Aunt Crystal nudged my shoulder with her elbow. "Haven't you seen a condo foyer before?"

She brushed by me and headed toward a mirrored wall with a huge marble counter like a hotel reception desk.

"Good afternoon, Miss Crystal." The gentleman behind the counter tipped his hat, came around the front of the desk, took the last grocery bag from her, and handed her a stack of mail. He could have been Santa's twin brother with his long, white fluffy beard, rosy cheeks, and twinkling eyes.

"And who do we have here?" He nodded politely toward me and stuck out his hand. His handshake was as strong as his English accent.

"This is my nephew Todd. He will be staying with me until Saturday. Todd, this is Norman."

She gave Norman her quick, raised-eyebrow smirk, and my stomach flip-flopped. The last time she smirked like that, vowel towels exploded with asparagus-eating aardvarks, incense-burning iguanas, and otters shucking oysters all over our bathroom floor!

Norman returned the smirk with a wink. "Welcome to the Applegate Plaza Condos at 115 Conjunction Ave., Todd. If you ever need anything, dial the front desk or, diggidy-dang-dong, just come and visit." He laughed, and his belly actually shook like a bowl full of jelly.

"Thank you, Norman." I liked him already.

"Miss Crystal." He turned to my aunt. "I tucked the minutes to last Thursday's condo meeting in with your mail."

I wandered off to explore while they talked. On my left were the gigantic glass doors to the front of the hotel, whoops, the condo. A whoosh of brisk cold air smacked my face as they opened and closed automatically when two oldie-goldies (ladies) left the building. To my right, hundreds of polished block shelves covered the lobby walls. Hmmm. Perfect for rock climbing. The shiny silver titanium and blue leather couch and lounge chairs looked like they came out of superhero Commander Hawk's spaceship. The lights above floated like asteroids. But the elevator in the middle of the lobby was old with black metal gates. It looked really out of place. It was like someone had forgotten to . . .

"That's the General Lee." A pizza delivery guy decked out in a red Totally Tasty Pizza hoodie and cap jarred me out of my observation.

"The General Lee?"

"Yes. We spell his name G-E-N-E-R-A-L-L-Y, but everyone just calls him The General. I'm Curt from Totally Tasty Pizza. You must be Todd. Your Aunt Crystal told me you would be staying with her this week."

Garummmmph. The heavy body of The General rumbled to a stop at the lobby and pulled my attention to its ancient doors that now clanked open. Oh no, the same parka girl from the parking garage slipped out through the General's prison-like metal door. I stepped behind a large palm tree so she couldn't see me. She headed toward a back hallway with a birdcage in her hand.

"You know her?" Curt nodded toward the parka girl.

"No." My answer slipped out too quickly to be believable. I stepped back around the tree and looked up. "A palm tree in the winter?"

As Curt launched into a lesson about tropical plants being good for better sleeping and breathing, my eyes wandered toward The General which was now opening again. An older, white-haired, fancy-schmancy woman waddled into view. The sparkly tiara plunked on top of her head caught my eye. With most of her fingers laced with gold rings, she gripped a shiny black purse in front of her big fur coat. Nestled in the pocket of her purse was a teeny weenie Chihuahua that also wore a dazzling tiara. Kind of like twins. Norman moved to greet her as she paraded toward us.

"Good afternoon, Mrs. Quigley and Miss Paris," Norman called.
"Have you met Miss Crystal's nephew, Todd?" But Mrs. Quigley did
an about-face and headed back to the elevator with a scowl.

As she swung her purse over her shoulder, Paris yelped mid-air. Then
Mrs. Quigley did the weirdest thing. She raised her right hand and held
it on the silver plate mounted to the right of the elevator gates. She
mumbled something and then turned toward us with a big fake smile.
Still grumbling, she swaggered past Norman toward the front door.

"I will never get used to that system. I have too many more important
matters on my mind." She grouched to everyone in earshot and headed
towards the sliding glass entryway that led onto the street.

"Oh, but what a great opportunity to sharpen your grammatical skills,"
Curt called after Mrs. Quigley.

"Don't you have some pizza to deliver, Curt?" Norman now stood
beside us and inhaled the wafts of warm cheese, onions, and ham.

"Oh yeah! Nice to meet you, Todd. I'll see you soon." He hurried
toward The General.

And then he did it too. Pizza bag held high above his head in his left
hand like you see in movies, Curt raised his right hand, plopped his
palm on the same plate to the right of the elevator doors, and mumbled

something. I barely heard him say, "Quickly or slowly . . ." as he disappeared into the rickety elevator.

"The General is quite active this afternoon." Norman tipped his hat in Aunt Crystal's direction as he headed back to his desk.

Aunt Crystal folded her mail and minutes in half and tucked them into the bag of groceries that now sat on Norman's desk.

"What does he mean? There's a system?" I ran around the front of Aunt Crystal to face her straight on with my question, but she pivoted around me now with grocery bag under her arm.

"You'll see." She winked at Norman.

Oh no.

Chapter Two

THE INSIDE OF THE elevator was just a wooden room with a weathered bench at the far end. Scratched and faded mirrors hung on the two side walls. It even smelled old and musty, like a Wild West saloon (not that I had been in one), but Aunt Crystal didn't seem to notice this rig was out of place in her fancy building. Above the wooden bench hung a large corkboard mounted in a gold-painted frame. A faded piece of paper with the word *Advertisements* written on it was pinned up with smiley face push-pins. Pretty low-tech for such a high tech-place. Wait. The bulletin board actually said *Adverbtisements*. I rolled my eyes. If these old people would just use computers, there wouldn't be any typos.

"Oh, silly me, I completely 🔔 forgot the birthday gift for my great niece's sixteenth birthday party this evening." Mrs. Quigley pushed through the closing elevator doors and almost clipped Paris's head. "I'm sorry to burst in like this, but I must immediately 🔔 head back to my condominium pronto. I can't be late for such an event. I will be the talk of the town if I darest be late. Teddy, be a dear, and quickly press floor number six for me, please."

Aunt Crystal winked as if to say, *don't worry about her getting your name wrong, she won't ever remember it.* Aunt Crystal nodded toward the panel of buttons.

I pushed the silver buttons for floors six and thirteen. They shone like someone had polished them a million times. Why did such an old elevator have such a modern panel? We had barely started moving, when I noticed that The General had already dinged as if we had gone past five or six floors. There was something strange about this elevator.

"Mrs. Quigley," Aunt Crystal scratched Paris under the chin, "You look like you're off to quite a party today."

"Oh yes, oh yes, for my niece, Francesca Isabella Margaret Ruby Lennox. She is a wonderful young lady with such great potential. She attends the Abernathy Academy for exceptional students. She has a 99.2% average currently. She's an exquisite six feet tall, quite bewitching when she strolls, with ravishing high cheekbones, long silky brown hair, and exquisite icy green eyes. Oh heavens, I actually just quoted the write-up directly from her modeling resume. Hoo-hoo-hoo-hoo-hoo. She's just 🔔 in town this weekend. It's her birthday, so I must get a visit in with her. I truly 🔔 hope she loves the blush rose watch I picked out for her sweet sixteen. I made sure that my jeweler crafted it with sixteen princess-cut diamonds. I'm sure 🔔 she'll just 🔔 love it. Oh. Here's my stop. Nice to meet you, Teddy."

Mrs. Quigley gave a little royal wave, headed to the right down the hall, and disappeared while she scolded Paris as if it was her fault she forgot the gift.

"That was exhausting." I stared at the numbers above the doors that now steadily progressed upwards. "She kind of 🔔 laughs like an owl. Hoo-hoo-hoo-hoo-hoo," I mimicked. I planned on avoiding Mrs. Quigley this week.

"What's with the dings, the lights, and the rumbling of the elevator floor? The dings don't match the number of floors that we passed. Is there something wrong with the electrical system? Maybe 🔔 we should have taken the stairs." I searched Aunt Crystal's face for answers.

My aunt's face looked like she just saw a giant spider wearing a tutu. "Walk up thirteen flights of stairs? Not 🔔 this old girl."

Yikes! I didn't want to do that either. "Well, maybe 🔔 Norman should call the repairman. I don't want to get stuck in here. It's not a new elevator and you never 〰 know what might happen. Deshaun told me that once 〰 he, two of his sisters, and a nurse got stuck in the hospital elevator for four hours. There was no food, no bathroom, and there were a lot of scary banging noises that came from below the floor. His little sister, Tonisha, kept farting-on-demand even though no-one was demanding it. The nurse started puking in her lunch bag because Tonisha smelled so 🔔 disgusting. And Deshaun had just 〰 chugged an extra-large Big Gulp and had to pee in a cup while 〰 his sisters stood in front him like a shield. Meanwhile, 〰 his older sister, Clove, found a bunch of insects in the corner of the drop-ceiling and started telling horror stories of insects burrowing in your hair and eating their way into your brain. And then 〰 . . ."

"We've arrived." Aunt Crystal pointed to the right as the elevator doors opened.

I bee-lined it out of the elevator as quickly as possible. I looked back and caught Aunt Crystal placing her hand on the silver plate outside and to the right of the doors as they clanked shut.

"Quickly or slowly, barely or wholly, tomorrow we will meet again."

"What was that for? Is that the system?"

"This way, Todd. Unit #1322."

"But you just said something about bears and holes and meeting up with someone tomorrow. What was that all about? Why did you do that? Is that what Mrs. Quigley and Curt said too?"

I scurried after Aunt Crystal, still juggling my duffle bag, grocery bags, and now a bunch of new questions.

"You're getting to know The General." Aunt Crystal smiled and slid a key card into the controlled lock on her condo door.

A deep, male, automated voice said, "Welcome, Miss Crystal. You have six new email messages and one voicemail message. A large number sixteen pizza with a stuffed crust will arrive in twenty-seven minutes."

"Quadruple whoa!" My duffle bag landed at my feet with a thud. "You have your own automated butler? That's awesome."

I snooped around while Aunt Crystal changed into comfy clothes. She had lots of bookshelves with lots and lots and lots of books. Tons about bees. Lots about honey. Stacks of paper piles almost hid the enormous desk in the den. The pictures on the walls were all bees, beehives, "Save the Bees" posters, and university degrees.

The TV in the living room was the size of a laptop though. She'd better have a bigger one than that somewhere else if I was stuck here all week. Her furniture was all antique stuff. The old dining room table had eight chairs all tucked in as if no one had used them in a hundred years. Except for the captain's chair at the end. It was loaded with a pile of science magazines. Glasses, spoons, honey bottles, Bunsen burners, salt, mustard, labels, and pens covered the table. What did she do in here? What did she burn? Exactly how did a Bunsen burner work? I held it high, revolved it, and tried to figure out how to turn it on.

"Find anything interesting?" Aunt Crystal joined me in the dining room, now sporting track pants and a Honeywell University sweatshirt. There were a few flies buzzing around her head. No, wait - those weren't flies!

"Duck!" Like lightning, I grabbed the closest magazine, rolled it up like a baseball bat, and started swinging. "Bees!"

"No, no, no!" Aunt Crystal grabbed my arm and stopped my swatting. "The bees are mine. They are my friends." She stuck out her hand so I would give her the magazine.

I froze. *Friendly bees?*

"Todd, I want you to meet Honey, Buzz Aldrin, and Frizzbee. Bee-u-ties meet Todd. I told them you'd be staying with us this week."

Honey flew close to my face and looked me straight in my eyes. She had very long eyelashes and a sweet smile. And she wore a tiny pair of granny glasses.

"Welcome, Todd," she said in a tiny, squeaky voice. She batted her eyelashes and fluttered away to sit on Aunt Crystal's shoulder.

Oh my goodness, this was crazy! Talking bees! I looked all over for the hidden camera and wondered if I was the newest target of Punk'd.

Buzz Aldrin circled my head and checked me out like a drill sergeant. He hovered in front of my nose. This one wasn't friendly. Every part of his thorax was muscular and tense. And his eyes were very serious. I would have to keep my eye on him.

"I don't think he likes me." I stiffened, afraid he might sting me.

"Give him some time. By the end of the week, you'll be friends."

Buzz gave me a *You're-free-to-go* nod and flew up to the top of a bookshelf. He landed on a book called *How to Recover from a Bee Sting,* and tapped his middle-leg abruptly. Was he trying to tell me something?

"Don't worry," Aunt Crystal rolled her eyes at Buzz. "Male bees don't have stingers. He's all talk."

Buzzzzzzzzzzzzzzzzzzzzzzzzzzzzzzzzzzzzzzzzzzzzzzzzz. I naturally brushed away at the buzzing tickle on my left ear.

"And this is Frizzbee. He likes attention."

Frizzbee circled my head three times as fast as he could, then landed on Aunt Crystal's outstretched hand. He teetered a little and then fell on his back.

"You silly boy. You're not dizzy." She tickled his belly with her pointer finger. "Bees also don't have an inner ear balance organ like we do, so they can't be dizzy," Aunt Crystal nodded in my direction. "He's quite an actor."

"Aunt Crystal, you just asked me if I found anything interesting. From the moment I stepped out of your car, there have been a hundred interesting things: cars for trillionaires, a spaceship foyer, and a wacky old elevator that makes noises, rumbles, and lights up like fireworks. There's some secret handshake with the elevator, modern door keys, an automated butler, cool science equipment, and now talking pet bees."

"So you didn't think Mrs. Quigley was interesting?" She snort-giggled.

"Wait till the guys hear about this."

Chapter Three

"MISS CRYSTAL, A PIZZA delivery person is in the front lobby requesting entry." The automated voice interrupted our condo tour.

Aunt Crystal squinted as she fidgeted with some buttons on a keyboard on the wall just inside the front door. "Aristotle, please let Curt in."

"The voice has a name?" I called after her as she scurried down the hall for her purse.

"Sure does. Aristotle was a Greek scientist, philosopher, and well-known bee-keeper from back in the 300s. I thought it fitting." Aunt Crystal dug through her wallet for cash and counted out a fist full of fives.

Knock, knock, knock.

Honey, Buzz, and Frizz whipped by my head in a race to the door. Frizz, a little out of control, crashed right into it. A little spin-ny, he bounced back and joined the other two at the peephole.

"The pizza is here, the pizza is here!" Honey announced in the tiniest, squeakiest voice ever.

Her eyelashes batted a hundred times a second as she headed straight for my face. Now nose to nose, she fluttered with excitement. "I love pizza with honey!"

Aunt Crystal opened the door, and there stood Curt smiling ear to ear. The smell of hot cheese and pepperoni filled the room.

"Hi, Miss Crystal." Curt reached into the black thermal pouch and handed her a steamy boxed pizza. "Hi, Todd. Told you I'd be back. Right on time. Hi, Honey. You look beautiful today."

Honey perched on my left shoulder, and hum-giggled in my ear.

"Did you drizzle honey on it this time?" Honey blushed a soft pink between her layers of yellow and black fur.

"Oh, I didn't forget." Curt leaned in to inspect Frizz's noggin now that Frizz had stopped loop-de-looping in excitement and had settled on the lip of an empty antique umbrella stand.

"You look like you have a bump on your head. Did you bang into the door again?"

Frizz wobbled a little, but took off and landed safely on the edge of Curt's hood.

"Silly bee. You be careful," he said to Frizz. "Remember, you fell asleep the last time I was here and fell right into my hood? I almost took you home by accident. Good thing you snore loudly."

"I bee-member," Frizz mumbled with a dizzy smile.

Buzz Aldrin gave his best Peter Pan pose, middle-leg perched on his mid-yellow stripe, on top of the large framed picture of Sherlock Holmes hung behind the door. Sherlock was covered head to toes with bees. Buzz tapped his tiny black foot while he tried to wait patiently for Curt to notice him.

Curt took off his pizza visor and saluted. "Well, hello Buzz. You are looking very important today. Is that why you're perched up there? The caption beneath Sherlock is a great one to memorize if you haven't already. *The little things are infinitely the most important.*"

Buzz flew to the bookshelf and struck up a super hero pose on top of a stack of books. On top was a VERY large book called *The Hungry Honey Bee*. Again, it seemed like Buzz was sending a message, but Curt didn't seem to notice.

Curt wiggled an enormous book out from underneath *The Hungry Honey Bee* and knocked Buzz flying. "Ooooh. This is one of my favorite books, Miss Crystal." Curt grinned as he pointed to the title on the spine. "*War and Peace.* Did you know that Leo Tolstoy, the author, was a beekeeper? Oh, of course you knew that. That comes to eighteen dollars, Miss Crystal." Curt held his hand out for the pizza payment.

"Todd, there's a flyer on top of the box you might want to look at." Curt tapped his finger on the crinkled sheet taped to the top of the box. "Totally Tasty Pizza has a contest right now where you can win pizza-for-a-year for you and your class. All you have to do is submit a Spring Break story on our website by this Friday to be entered to win." Curt shot a gleaming white smile and wiggled his eyebrows.

"Me, write a Spring Break story?" I clutched my chest. "That's not really my thing."

"Give it some thought, Todd. Miss Crystal tells me you're a smart kid and thinks you have a pretty excellent shot at winning. But you only have till Friday."

Curt re-shelved *War and Peace* and turned to leave. I could see that tucked inside his thermal pouch was a second pizza box with the name *A. Patel* written in magic marker on the side. It had to be Awish in the robin-egg-blue parka. I can't bump into her this week. It's hard not to look at her scarred and twisted mouth when you talk to her, and she's sometimes hard to understand. I should have stayed at Deshaun's.

"I've never had pizza drizzled with honey before." I tried to steer the subject away from Spring Break stories as I followed Aunt Crystal into the living room.

Aunt Crystal carried in the pizza. "I hope you're OK if we just eat in front of the TV tonight."

"Sure. Do you want to watch a Sherlock Holmes movie? You must like him." I nodded towards the giant picture at the front door.

"You know he's a famous beekeeper, don't you?"

"I would have never guessed," I announced with my best British accent, dropped in front of the tiny TV, and looked for the remote.

"Aristotle, release the Kraken!" Aunt Crystal gave her best Zeus impersonation and plopped down on the couch, nowhere near the laptop-sized TV.

A low-pitched rumble grew louder and louder and louder. I gasped as the bare living room wall completely transformed into a massive home theater system. It had to be ten feet long and eight feet high . . . no joke!

"Wait till the guys hear about this."

Tuesday

"**G**OOD MORNING, MASTER TODD and Miss Crystal." Aristotle's voice startled me as I dragged myself down the hall toward the smell of bacon. "It is Tuesday, March thirteenth. It is a chilly thirty-six degrees outside. Just a reminder that the rooftop landing happens at 9:45 a.m. It is advised that Miss Honey, Master Buzz Aldrin, nor Master Frizz-bee should attend due to the wind chill factor and elevated velocity.

I plopped down at the breakfast table and finished buttoning up my lucky flannel shirt. Black and yellow, just like the Seattle Sting colors. I rubbed my chest for good luck. Fingers crossed it'll bring something cool to do this week.

"Morning, Punkinhead," Aunt Crystal flipped some sizzling bacon strips.

"Hey, my mom calls me that."

"I just wanted you to feel like you were at home this week. Did you hear Aristotle?"

"Yeah, what's the roof top landing?"

"Oh, I think you better do some exploring to find out. I have a video call around that time, so I won't be able to join you. But make sure you take your phone so you can get a good shot and maybe some video. You won't want to miss it."

I looked around. "Hey where are your bee friends? I thought they would be awake by now."

"Oh, they're awake." She nodded toward the window ledge.

Frizz laid on his back while tears streamed down onto the windowsill. Honey's eyes, as well, filled with monster-sized drops that dripped all over her yellow body hair. Out of the corner of my eye, I saw Buzz fly in with a tiny piece of tissue for Honey's leaky eyes. But with a glint in his big worker-bee eyes, his second air drop released a tissue that covered Frizz's whole body.

"What's up, you guys? Why are you so sad?"

Frizz sat up, but all I could hear was the muffle of his nasal voice underneath the sheet of tissue.

Honey whipped the tissue off Frizz with her spindly bee legs, dabbed his eyes, and gave him a big hug. "We never get to see the landing, Todd." She turned to Aunt Crystal, who was now loading strips of bacon on a plate. "We promise to stay inside the building, Miss Crystal. We promise. We won't go outside. We triple promise."

All three swooped in unison and huddled side-by-side on the spice rack beside the stove. Kneeling on their itty bitty teeny weenie bees knees, they begged Aunt Crystal to let them go (It seemed appropriate that Honey knelt on cinnamon, Frizz on cajun spice, and Buzz on the red hot chili pepper bottle).

"Oh, how can I refuse those faces? As long as Todd wants to go see the helicopter and promises to keep an eye on you, then yes. You can go."

"A helicopter? Landing on top of your building?" I felt my eyes bug out so much that I thought they would fall out. "I'm definitely in."

"I thought you might be." Aunt Crystal's eyes twinkled. "But absolutely no letting these guys outside of the rooftop viewing atrium, or we will never see them again. Then I would be the one sitting on the window ledge crying." Aunt Crystal wagged her pointer finger at her small friends.

In all the excitement, Frizz slipped off his jar, fell thorax-first into the tiny black railing of the spice rack, and got his head stuck. Honey stopped midway through her jitterbug celebration to pull Frizz out of his crisis. But Buzz took flight, doing three loop-dee-loops, and landed on the tea towel that hung from the refrigerator door. Printed in the middle of the towel was the word *Merci*. Once again, I was pretty sure this bee was trying to say something.

Honey, Buzz, and Frizz fluttered toward Aunt Crystal. They planted butterfly kisses on her cheeks while she set down plates of hot buttered toast, scrambled eggs, and bacon at the dining room table.

I could barely eat my breakfast because I was already off in La-la land. All I could think was that a helicopter was going to land only feet away from me. Maybe the pilot would offer me a ride. Maybe he'd let me fly it for a bit. Maybe I'd save someone's life. I'd be in the newspaper. I'd get a medal from the Mayor. Just wait till the guys heard this.

Aunt Crystal slipped something into my shirt pocket as my new friends made a beeline (ha ha *bee-line*, sometimes I'm pretty funny) to the door at 9:30 a.m. "You may need this." She cracked a smile.

Unsure of what I was to do once I stepped into The General, I ignored what I had seen the day before and just walked on board the old

28

rickety elevator. Buzz chest-bumped the button for the rooftop floor with his abdomen. All three bees perched on my shoulder and waited. There was a bump and a bit of movement, but not much. I looked at my favorite superhero (Commander Hawk) G-Brain watch and waited.

"This old elevator better not give up the ghost now."

The elevator moved an inch. Buzz got impatient and dove into my pocket. *Muffle muffle grunt shuffle muffle.* He wiggled back out and then he flew up to my face with a piece of paper between his teeth. He hovered in front of my eyes.

I took the slip of paper. "What's this? It's a list of words. Silly, quietly, away, tomorrow, never, well, slowly, cheerfully, bravely, upstairs, boldly, outside, finally, badly, warmly, afterwards."

The General started to really move, ding, rumble, and flash!

"Keep reading, Todd!" Honey buzzed around in circles full of smiles. "Keep reading! This is fun!"

"Always, sometimes, rudely, only, so, hard, fast, wildly, often, weekly, before, nearby, today, downstairs, yesterday, soon, seldom."

"Faster, 🔔 Todd, faster!" 🔔 Honey spun like a top. Frizz bumped from one wall to the next to the next. The elevator lights blinked wildly like a disco ball.

"Happily, 🔔 slowly, 🔔 since, 〰 now, 〰 before, 〰 behind." 💥

Buzz flitted in front of my face with angry bee eyes. I guess all the flashing, sounds, and shaking was over-the-top for him. I stopped reading. The elevator slowed. The lights stopped. The rumbling stopped.

"That was weird 🔔 and cool 🔔 at the same time. I guess we're here." 💥

The doors chugged open, and Buzz marched (as much as one can while flying) straight ahead and hovered over the sign on the glass doors that said *Observation Deck. Do not open doors during landing.*

I followed Buzz, but halted at the entrance of the rooftop. "Whoa, my knees feel a little weak. We're up REALLY high."

I backed away from the glass doors and stood closer to the solid brick wall beside the elevator. I was in the perfect spot. I could see the landing pad about a hundred feet away. I tried not to look beyond the edge of the building.

"Whoa, I don't know how Commander Hawk flies this high!"

"Pretty lights, pretty lights, Todd," Frizz floated aimlessly around the landing count-down clock above the sliding glass doors to the landing deck. "1:30, 1:29, 1:28, 1:27, 1:26, 1:25, 1:24 . . ."

Buzz, annoyed at Frizz's counting, dove through Frizz's wobbly flight and landed on the bright red "stop" light next to the countdown clock. He bee-growled at Frizz to let him know what he thought of his countdown.

Just then, the sliding glass doors swooshed open with a huge blast of chilly March air. Buzz held on for dear life to the corner of the light box. I quickly dove towards the big *CLOSE* button and immediately pressed it to prevent Buzz from being swept away. Unexpectedly, someone slipped through the doors.

Frantically, I grabbed for Buzz and searched for Frizz and Honey. Thankfully, they had already tucked themselves away safely in my shirt pocket. Buzz dove in to join them. Each stuck their head above the upper stitching of my pocket to see who it was.

"It's Awish! Hi Awish," Honey slipped first out of my pocket to greet Awish with butterfly kisses on her chilly cheek.

"Awish the Fish?" I whispered. Me and my dense brain. I knew right away that it was wrong to call her that, but it just sort of slipped out.

Buzz stormed out of the warm flannel pocket on my chest and hovered nose to nose with me. With his arms crossed, shoulders back, and black eyes glaring, he made it clear that he was not pleased with the name I had just called his friend.

Awish Patel was brand new in my grade three class at Brevda Heights. Rumor was she had some sort of accident that made her mouth look that way, which might also be the reason she now lived alone with her grandmother. Her teeth poked out all sides of her mouth and her lips puckered like a fish. At school, Awish chose to eat her lunch in the Counselor's office because she was embarrassed when food dropped from her mouth.

"Awish, what are you doing here?" I hoped she hadn't heard my stupid remark.

"Hi Todd," Awish pulled her pink plaid scarf up over her mouth as much as she could. "My grandmother is landing in, wow, less than twenty seconds. I try to meet her as often as I can. She's away on business a lot. What are you doing here?"

"Your grandmother? She travels by helicopter? I'm staying with my aunt this week while my parents and sister are away."

"Oh, Miss Crystal must be your aunt if you're hanging with Frizz, Honey, and Buzz. She's a really smart lady. She has been helping me with my science homework since I moved here." Awish turned quickly toward the big glass windows and pointed. "I think I see Nani coming!"

Awish bounced up and down and waved like a windmill at the sight of the helicopter. Honey, Buzz, and Frizz bopped up and down too . . . although it's a known fact that bees can't jump.

The big yellow chopper lowered slowly, with great precision, onto the top of the building. It was so close that the observation deck windows shook. The bright yellow machine stood still, but large, frightening blades continued to whip around and around. A second, but much smaller, set of blades at the tail of the helicopter slowed. I was sure I didn't want to be any closer than this. Those blades looked like they could hurt someone.

"Just wait till the guys hear about this."

Frizz, in the excitement of seeing the helicopter so closely, bumped into the glass window. We all laughed when we watched him slide down on to the ledge.

"Oh, you silly bee." Awish scooped him up into her palm. "So, Miss Crystal finally let you come to see the helicopter land, huh?" She held Frizz high enough to talk nose to nose, but she still draped her scarf over her mouth. "You must have been a good boy."

Frizz tossed his head to the side, acting shy.

"Back in my pocket, everyone! The doors are going to open." I stepped closer to the wall beside The General and watched. A man who looked like he was a secret agent for the Defenders of the Earth, one of Commander Hawk's sidekicks, helped Awish's grandmother out of the helicopter. She gripped her briefcase in front of her heavy winter coat and ducked as she made her way towards the glass entryway.

Thud, thump, clop. Mrs. Patel stomped the snow and slush off her black leather boots as she burst through the glass doors. "Well, that was refreshing!"

Mrs. Patel was a beautiful woman. Her smile was brilliant white and outlined by bright red lipstick. And her hair bounced back into a perfect mess of black curls as she shook off the traces of snow that had nestled in her hair.

"First order of the day," Mrs. Patel began. "Where is my hug?" She held out her arms towards Awish and squeezed her tight. "And I see you have brought friends today. Hello Honey, Buzz, and Frizz. What an honor to have you welcome me home. And who else have you brought with you?"

"Nani, this is Todd. We are in the same class at school, and he is staying with his Aunt Crystal this week," Awish said, stretching her arm towards me.

"Hello Todd. Welcome to the Applegate Plaza Helipad." Mrs. Patel removed her mirrored black sunglasses.

I was a little entranced by her beautiful eyes. "Nice to meet you, ma'am," I reached out to shake her hand.

"And a gentleman as well, I see." Mrs. Patel removed her gloves and gave me a firm handshake.

"Wop-wop-wop-wop-wop-wop," chanted Frizz as his little head tried to keep in rhythm of the circling tail blades of the chopper.

Everyone laughed as Frizz started to fall. He was pretending to be dizzy again. I caught him on the way down.

"I think you should just slip in here for now." I tucked Frizz back into my shirt pocket. "I saw your car in the parking garage. It's lit." I said to Mrs. Patel.

"Lit. Hmmmm, that means you like it, right?" Mrs. Patel cocked her head at me and then towards Awish.

"Yes, Nani." Awish giggled at Nani's question while still hiding her mouth under her scarf. "*Lit* means the same thing as when you say *cool*."

"Ah." She nodded when she understood. "You must like fast things, like helicopters and Bugattis."

"I do, but I'd never been this close to either till now. Mrs. Patel, my Aunt Crystal says she hasn't met you yet, but you know her bee-friends?"

"Quite right." Mrs. Patel walked toward the elevator and pushed the button. "Awish ba-bee sits these bee-auties when your Aunt Crystal is away." She winked at the three friends peering out over the hem of Todd's chest pocket. "Your Aunt Crystal and I will need to make a date to get to know each other. Awish says that your aunt has been helping her with her science and that she is a brilliant woman."

I waited for her to put her hand on the plate to the right of the elevator door and say something about being fast and holy like the others when they got on The General, but she didn't.

"Buzz, would you do the honor of pushing floor number twenty for me?" Mrs. Patel asked as we stepped inside the elevator.

"Nani, there is a contest that I am hoping to win this week," Awish began. "I can win pizza for a year for my class if I write a Spring Break story for Totally Tasty Pizza."

"Work hard. Be unique. And bring home the win for you and your class!" Nani's eyes gleamed. "Todd, it was a pleasure meeting you. Do you like hockey?"

36

"I sure 🔔 do!"

"Well, perhaps 〰 you would like to come to a game with us some time. We cheer for the Seattle Sting."

"The Seattle Sting! That's my favorite team! I would love to go to a game! Do *you* like hockey, Mrs. Patel?"

"Todd, I love hockey so 🔔 much 🔔 I bought the team!" she laughed. "And I named them after the best animal in the world." Then she winked at Frizz, fist-bumped Buzz, and tickled Honey under her chin as she and Awish got off the elevator at floor number twenty, arm in arm.

"Whoa," I gulped.

"Wait till the guys hear about this?" Honey chanted.

"Hey." I felt the heat creep up my neck into my cheeks. She was mimicking me.

Wednesday

"OH, YOU SCARED ME!" Awish gasped as she stepped into The General and practically flipped over me as I laid on the floor. "What are you doing down there?" She pushed the Lobby button and automatically covered her mouth with the notebook she carried.

"Hi, Awish." I sat up. I still had that sick feeling in my stomach from yesterday's Awish-the-Fish blunder.

"I'm trying to figure out what's up with this elevator. It flashes, rumbles, and lights up. It doesn't make any sense. People say some sort of magic words either before they get in or when they get out, and I don't know why. The bees and I got in yesterday, morning when we were going to watch your grandmother land. The only thing that seemed to make this old elevator move was when I started reading a list of words that Aunt Crystal put in my pocket. But when your grandmother got in the elevator she didn't say or do anything, but she got to her floor. It just doesn't make sense."

Awish plopped down on the old bench near the back of The General. She swung her legs around and rested them on the bench. She opened her notebook and grabbed a neon pink pen from the spine of the book and started writing. She tugged her turtleneck up over her chin and mouth.

"What are you doing?" I asked.

"I'm going to win pizza-for-a-year for our class," she said confidently, and continued to work.

"Have you ever eaten honey on pizza?" I broke the silence.

"I've never tried that before." She giggled and tugged up the turtleneck sweater again. "Have you?"

"We had it last night. It was Honey's idea. It was pretty good. Strange, but good."

"I always order mango and pineapple on mine," she replied.

"Mango? I've heard of pineapple on pizza, but never mango."

"You'll have to try it when I win this contest," she giggled and set her notebook and pen on the bench. The General stopped moving. We had arrived at the lobby.

"I'll be back. ❃ I have to pick up the mail for Nani. Hold the elevator?" She tugged at her turtleneck again to ensure it was over her mouth, and headed out into the lobby.

Hold the elevator? I didn't even know how to run this thing. Thankfully, she was back in a flash.

"No mail." She curled up on the bench with knees folded up almost to her chest. She retrieved her notebook and pen and wrote again.

"Do you want me to push a floor for you?"

"No thanks. I'll just work right ❃ here."

"Say that again."

"Say what?"

"What you just said."

"No thanks. I'll just work right ❃ here?"

"Right, ❃ right, ❃ right." ❃ I tested the elevator. I stood up and pushed floor number thirteen. The elevator moved.

Awish joined in, "Right, ❃ right, ❃ right." ❃

And the elevator went faster. We laughed at our discovery. The
elevator door opened at floor thirteen, but we just let it close again and
continued with our experiment.

"Say something else," I urged her.

"I'm having surgery today soon. 〰 Cool! We got a new one!"

"Really?" 🔔 I turned and stared at her.

"Yeah, didn't you feel it rumble?"

"No, I mean, are you really 🔔 having surgery today soon 〰 or was
that just totally 🔔 random?"

"Oh yeah, that. Yeah, my grandmother will come to get me very 〰
shortly." 〰

Awish hid her face in her notebook and pretended to write. She
ignored the rumbles that interrupted the awkwardness in the elevator.
She looked scared.

"What did you say to make that happen?" I changed the subject.

"My grandmother will come to get me very 〰 shortly. 〰 Isn't *very*
〰 an adverb? I think *shortly* 〰 is an adverb too." She wrote it down
in her book.

The elevator stood still. There was no movement, even though there were two rumbles. I climbed on top of the end of the bench that Awish sat on. I checked the corners of the elevator. I inspected the ceiling. I jumped down on my hands and knees and found a small 6" x 16" metal door with a ring handle underneath the bench.

"Look." I waved Awish over to check it out. "It's a hidden meter. It's got to measure three things because there are three gauges."

Knelt on the floor beside me, Awish sketched the meter in her notebook. "Probably 🔔 one that makes the elevator rumble, one that makes it flash, and then one that makes it ding."

She dropped her head and went back to write madly in her book again.

"That's it, Awish! You're right. We are getting really 🔔 close!" I high-fived her, which was a little awkward because I was becoming friends with a girl, and not just any girl . . . a girl that I had been embarrassed to be friends with at school. What would the guys think? I shoved that thought aside. "Let's keep working at this. We're going to solve this mystery."

"And we're going to win the pizza-for-a-year for our class!" Awish crawled back on the bench and scribbled some more.

"Well, maybe 🔔 you are. Not me. Writing isn't my thing," I huffed and went back to the meter; this time taking pictures with my phone.

Not a moment later, The General kicked into gear and started moving upwards.

"Must be time for me to go. It looks like we're heading to floor number twenty. Todd, I need you to do me a favor, but you MUST pinky swear you won't tell anyone about my secret project." Awish held up her pinky to lock with mine.

"Pinky swear? What kind of favor, first?"

"You promise you won't tell anyone?"

"Hand over my heart, Scouts honor, promise." I jumped to stand at attention with my hand over my heart and three fingers in the air with my left hand. No pinky swears for me.

"I need you to take care of the APVC," Awish began, but the elevator door opened, and she stopped speaking.

Mrs. Patel stood there holding a small overnight bag and Awish's robin egg blue winter parka. "I thought I might find you here."

She stepped into the elevator, offered both sleeves open to Awish, and helped her zip up the front. "Good morning, Todd." Mrs. Patel nodded in my direction with a forced smile. "It's time to go, dear." She winced at Awish and then turned gracefully toward the elevator doors, looked up at the floor numbers, and side hugged Awish. "Let's do this," she said.

I wasn't sure if Mrs. Patel was talking to herself or Awish. I saw a trickle of a tear in the corner of her eye.

"Quickly 🔔 or slowly, 🔔 barely 🔔 or wholly, 🔔 tomorrow 〰 we will meet again." 〰 Mrs. Patel recited it as if she had to while she stared straight ahead. She didn't want to talk.

The three of us stood in silence. Awish really was going for surgery.

When the doors opened, I quickly glanced at Awish, who had her head down. She looked super freaked out. "You can't go. We almost 〰 have this elevator mystery cracked. And you've got to finish the Spring Break story."

"I'll only 〰 be gone a couple of days." Her lips trembled. She tried to smile and zipped up her parka over her mouth. "You figure it out and I'll finish the Spring Break story while 〰 I'm in the hospital." She crossed her heart. "And don't forget the APVC," she whispered, and handed me a small white envelope.

"A couple of days?" I tucked the envelope into my jacket pocket. The General's door closed, and they were gone. I stood stunned.

Thursday

"MISS CRYSTAL, THERE IS an in-coming phone call from an unknown number," Aristotle announced early Thursday morning. Aunt Crystal rose from the kitchen table where I picked through my Flake-e-o's. She headed toward the phone in the den.

"Good morning, Crystal speaking."

Frizz and Honey squatted on the edge of the sugar bowl in front of me, and tried to cheer me up. "What's buzzing you, Todd?" Frizz asked sleepily.

"I guess I'm worried about Awish. She looked so scared yesterday, and I didn't want her to go. We were so close to solving the mystery of The General. I was even thinking about helping her with the essay because, well, you know, I love pizza."

"You can still do that," Honey fluttered her eyelashes. "We can help you."

Bang! A book fell high from one of the old dusty bookshelves in the living room. I jumped out of my skin! Buzz fluttered over it, whistling and looking into the air all innocent-like. I pushed back from the table and stooped to pick up the book and to scold Buzz for scaring everyone. But then I realized it was a book called *Schoolhouse Rock,* and it was open to a page titled *Lolly lolly lolly, Get your Adverbs here.*

"You're one smart little drone." I grinned at my crusty little friend.

Buzz set me back on track. I smacked the book closed and grabbed my cell phone. "Come on guys, we have work to do before Awish gets back."

"Speaking of Awish, that was her grandmother on the phone." Aunt Crystal relayed the message as my team stopped in its tracks at the door. "Her surgery took four hours. She is resting and seems to be healing well. She's still a little groggy, but she wanted you to know that she still plans on winning the contest, and that you better figure out the elevator by the time she's home."

"We plan on it, don't we, guys? We're the Bee-Team!" The three bee-uties dove in to meet my fist bump with their forewings. "All for one and one for all!" I headed to the door with cell phone in hand.

"Out of order?" Honey squeaked as she read the large white sheet of paper taped outside of The General's gates. "Oh no, what are we going to do?"

"Only for two hours." Frizz pointed to the small print with his wing.

"Guess we'll take the stairs." I marched down the hallway. "You guys are lucky. You can just fly."

We reached the first floor and saw that the elevator doors were wide open. An orange cone sat outside, letting us know the elevator was definitely not working. Inside the doorway, a man in a blue work uniform laid on the floor. Half of him was inside the elevator, and half was outside. Next to him, a toolbox sat by his legs. His body was twisted just enough that we couldn't see his face. Maybe he had been checking out the secret meter.

We hid around the corner just close enough that we could see and hear what was going on.

Suddenly, the body flopped to the right, then to the left, then to the right again. An older man with a heavy black mustache sat up. "Well, 🔔 you were right 🔔 to call me. The Adverbometer is low on pretty 🔔 well 🔔 every level. We must upgrade the power so that The General can remain operational."

"Adverbowhatter?" Frizz buzzed in a frenzy around my face.

"There's someone in there with the man on the floor, but they are out of my sight," I whispered to my friends. I hushed the bees so I could start recording on my phone app.

"Is it that serious, Guido?" the voice asked.

"That's Norman's voice," I mouthed to my team.

"The adverbometer," Guido swatted a bug that flew by his nose, "measures the rumbles, the lights, and the bell sounds. They create the electrical current to run the motor so the governor can move the elevator at a perfect speed. If there aren't enough rumbles, lights, and dings, then there isn't enough ⌇ power to move The General."

Buzz flew right into Todd's ear and whispered in a gruff drone voice. "I don't believe him. I did a fly-by. He says his name is Guido, but his hard hat and uniform says Otis."

"So, how do we fix it?" Norman sounded concerned.

"Three ways to fix the problem," Guido went on. "One: you get your condo owners serious about filling up the adverbometer. Two: you pay a company big 🔔 bucks to fill up the adverbometer, or Three: you get a new elevator."

50

"Oh my, option three sounds very 🔔 expensive." Norman sighed.

"Norman, the levels are quite 🔔 low. I would say that you have about a week left before The General gives out unless your condo residents get serious about their part in empowering him." Guido locked the meter door, got to his feet, and grabbed the pylon and tool box.

"Keep me posted," was the last thing we heard Guido say as I pushed *stop record* and we ducked into the stairway.

"Guys, we need to help save The General." I ran up the stairs two by two as the bees buzzed ahead of me. Exhausted by the time I reached the thirteenth floor, I choked out, "Whoa, we really need to save the elevator. If I can barely run all those stairs, then Aunt Crystal and the others could never do that. Let's get to work." I led our squad back to unit number 1322.

"I thought you guys were going to help me solve the case?" I yelled to Frizz, Buzz, and Honey as I shut the condo door. I checked in the warm dryer, rummaged through the freshly cut flowers on the dining room table, and even searched the bowl of smelly bath salts on the edge of the tub. "Where are you guys?"

"Behind the front door, Todd." Frizz circled in front of my face then led me to where the three sat all nestled on top of a flowery comforter in a heap below the Sherlock Holmes picture.

"What are you doing here?"

"This is where Aunt Crystal does her best thinking–right under Sherlock's nose," Honey squeaked.

I flopped down beside them and tapped my temples. Think, think, think. Honey, Buzz, and Frizz sat beside me and tapped their temples as well.

I started to list the clues on my fingers . . .

"Guido said that The General runs on adverbs. When people get in The General, they need to talk with adverbs to make it run. But what if the condo people don't know their adverbs?"

"Hey, what about the sign that said Adverbtisements? You took a picture of that yesterday." Frizz nudged my shoulder.

I looked at the picture on my phone. All the adverbs on the sign were underlined.

- Nellie's Nearly New Clothing - <u>gently</u> used clothing donations are <u>greatly</u> appreciated.

- Even-Keeled Boating Lessons - sign up <u>quickly</u>, before it is <u>too</u> late.

- <u>Happily</u> Ever After Book Club - <u>freely</u> accepting new members, <u>right</u> today.

- <u>Very</u> Vegan Take Out – <u>deliciously</u> vegan options 133 Seldom Street 519-344-4046

- Delia's Daily Dance Lessons - downstairs in the Yoga Studio at 7:00 p.m. <u>every</u> evening.

"Someone must have posted these so people could read them out loud to get The General moving. But that's obviously not working." I pointed to finger number two. "There have to be three types of adverbs if The General flashes, rumbles, and dings. And there were three gauges on the hidden meter too."

I scrambled to grab a yellow-lined scratchpad and pen from the dining room table and headed back to work with my friends. I wrote three headings on the notepad:

Adverbs that tell *how*

Adverbs that tell *where*

Adverbs that tell *when*

Honey took off toward the guest room and returned with the note Aunt Crystal had put in my pocket yesterday.

"That's awesome, Honey. Thanks."

Honey eyes sparkled. "You're welcome. I'm always happy to help."

I listed those alongside the ones from the sign inside The General as well.

"Come on, guys! Let's go try something." Jumping up too quickly, I accidentally sent Buzz hurling through the air after he'd nicely fallen asleep on my notepad.

Startled out of his slumber, Buzz's wing muscles let out a whop, whop, whop, warning sound. He was mad.

"Sorry about that, Buzz! I think I figured it out! Let's go!"

"He did it, he did it, he did it," Honey sang sweetly and followed over my right shoulder.

"Woo-hoo!" squealed Frizz. "What did he do?" He giggled and followed.

"I think I figured out how The General can be fixed! We don't need a new elevator. We need the condo people to use more adverbs! We need to fill the adverbometer! First one to the elevator gets a gigantic piece of baklava!"

"What's baklava?" Honey squeaked out as we raced Buzz and Frizz to the elevator.

The condo door slammed shut as we rounded the corner and headed toward The General.

"First!" I smacked my hands on the gates and pushed the button, and hoped I beat my friends to the elevator.

"First, first, first," came from each bee as they belly-landed on a floor number above The General at the same time.

"You don't know what baklava is? It is the most amazing dessert ever! And it is dripped with so much honey that you'll think you might need a lifeguard to rescue you."

"Honey?" The three dreamily hummed together. "We love honey."

"I wish Awish was here," I sighed.

"I wish Awish, ha-ha-ha-ha-ha-ha-ha," Frizz loop-de-looped a few times while we waited for The General to arrive at their floor. "That is so fun to say."

"Text her." Buzz grumbled, and then took a trip to the full-length mirror directly across from The General to flex his muscles. "Looks like we're going to be waiting a while, anyway."

I tapped out a message to Awish. The elevator doors opened, and there was no one inside. "Phew, glad there's no one in here. Come on, you guys." I took my list of adverbs out of my pocket.

"Let's see. Adverbs that tell how: slowly, ⌂ fast, ⌂ boldly, ⌂ rudely, ⌂ very." ⌂

"You've got it, Todd." Frizz loop-de-looped over my head, dancing to the dings.

Buzz knelt in front of the adverbometer box under the bench and gave a big thumbs-up.

"Buzz, which meter suddenly ⌂ filled up when I said those words?"

Buzz peered out from underneath the bench and held his breath till his face went blue.

"Excellent work, Buzz. The blue one fills up when we use adverbs that answer *how*." I jotted that in my notes. "What about these words, Buzz? Upstairs, ✸ out, ✸ downstairs, ✸ here?" ✸

"Oh Buzz," Honey pretended to faint when Buzz bent over and let one rip.

"Green gas for adverbs that say *where*. Very ⌂ creative, Buzz," I doubled over like a pretzel in laughter (not that pretzels laugh), and made my final deduction. "That means red for adverbs that say *when*."

"Let's get ready to r-u-m-b-l-e!" Frizz yelled as he cannon-balled from the bench onto Buzz's back.

"Do it, Todd. Say them. Say them. I love the rumble," Honey begged.

"Tomorrow, ⌁ never, ⌁ later, ⌁ soon, ⌁ finally." ⌁

Buzz shook Frizz off his back and turned red with anger.

"Excellent, Buzz." I thought Buzz had just confirmed that the red gauge was for the adverbs that say *when*, but then I realized he really was mad. I had to stop the wrestling match between the two. "Come on, guys. We've got this figured out. We need to let Awish know."

"You should let her know how 🔔 the APVC is going too," 🔔 Honey reminded me as The General's doors opened again and we headed back to the condo.

"The what?"

"The white envelope that Awish gave you to before she left for the hospital. You were supposed to look after the APVC while she was gone."

"How did you know about that?"

"She's my BFF. She tells me everything. And," Honey fluttered her lashes, "She asked me to make sure you didn't forget."

Back in Aunt Crystal's condo, I searched my jacket pockets for the envelope. What was the APVC? What did Awish want me to do? I had completely forgotten. I found the envelope in yesterday's jeans and ripped it open.

Dear Todd,

I'll only be gone a couple of days, but I need you to take care of the Applegate Plaza Vet Clinic while I'm gone. It's just outside the observation doors on the roof in a small greenhouse-type building. That's where I was coming from when I met you the day Nani's helicopter landed. No one knows it's there except Nani, Norman, and our chauffeur. I need you to feed, water, and do what's on each of my patients's cage. They're counting on you. If you fill up the bowls, then you only need to go once.

Please keep this as our secret.

Thanks,

Awish

I threw on my coat and ran to the elevator. I held my hand on the silver plate outside the door and recited, "Quickly or slowly, barely or wholly, tomorrow we will meet again." Proud that I remembered the ditty, I ran inside and pushed the shiny button that said *roof top.*

"Fast, 🔔 fast, 🔔 fast, 🔔 fast, 🔔 now, 〰 now, 〰 now, 〰 now, 〰 here, ✹ here, ✹ here, ✹ here, ✹ here." ✹

The doors opened so slowly it felt like I was watching worms do the 100-yard dash.

I ran to the rooftop automated sliding glass doors. "Come on, come on. Quicker, please!" Even those doors seemed to take forever to open. But when they finally did, the whoosh of the cold winter air stole my breath like I was stuck at the top of the Great American Scream Machine at Six Flags. I pulled my hood tight around my face and slipped outside. There was a warm yellow glow coming from the little building nestled around the corner from a pool house. Wait, there's a swimming pool up here?

My knees shook as I ran. Don't look at the edge of the building, don't look over, don't look down. I reached the glasshouse, unlatched the door, and stepped into the safe, warm building. All eyes were on me — all sorts of eyes were on me.

"Whoa." There had to be a dozen cages of small critters. Most were empty, but some held the little patients Awish mentioned in her letter. I took down my hood, so I didn't scare them.

"Well, hello, little girl," I opened the cage labeled *Holly*. "I've never held a hedgehog before. Don't be scared," I gently caressed the soft, spiky little pet. "Awish's note says you need your infected tooth brushed with this special cream. And then you can have a treat of dried crickets." I spoke with the tiniest, most caring voice I could muster up. "I guess I just goop the cream on this cotton swab." So, I went to work.

"And who do we have here?" I scooped up a bunny named Bingo two cages down. "Well, hello, Bingo. And how are you today? Oh, I see you have the snuffles, which makes you cough, sneeze, and grind your teeth. Dr. Awish (I laughed to myself) has prescribed this antibiotic for you." I picked up the small tube of cream that laid in a sterile tray beside his cage. "But the note says I'm supposed to sing a verse of *Little Rabbit Foo Foo*, or you won't take your medicine. I'm not very good at singing, but I'll give it a shot."

I gave my best rendition of the song while I gave Bingo his medicine.

"No telling Awish about my singing." I wagged my finger at Bingo and moved onto Itsy's cage.

I reached in to the cage and tried to find Itsy somewhere under all the shredded paper bits. The wheel in the cage made me think that Itsy might be a mouse. "I hope you weren't listening to the song I just sang to Bingo. Don't be afraid. I won't hurt you." I continued to rustle through the shavings. "I didn't mean a word of it." The song was about a little mouse getting bopped on the head. "Hey, where are you? Are you sleeping?" I swished my hand under all the cozy nest paper and found the tiniest little mouse ever.

"Oh no, Itsy." I held him up close to my face in both hands. "You have a broken nose and a crushed mouth. You must have been snooping around a mouse trap. But you must've been super fast to trick that old mouse trap, 'cause it looks like only your nose and mouth got stuck! Dr. Awish's notes say that you need some salve rubbed gently on your nose and lips, but I need to be careful because you're a biter!"

I avoided being bitten and moved on to re-bandage Elliott, the goldfinch's broken beak and Sssssssssam, the garter snake's sliced chin. I dropped a few flakes of fish food into Princess Pucker-up's bowl and noticed a fish hook leaning against the bowl. The note beside it said *Removed February twenty-second.*

"Ouch, you poor thing," I leaned over to whisper into the bowl. "You'll be better in no time."

I headed to the next cage and skidded to a stop.

"You've got to be kidding me!" I whispered louder than I should have.

There staring me in the face was a skunk! Terrified to go near that cage, I grabbed the note from as far away as I could reach.

A dog attacked Uncle Skunk, and his mouth wounds are healing slowly. Be calm. Dab his wounds with a fresh washcloth damp with soap and warm water. Spot a bit of ointment on his gash, and above all else . . . don't scare him or you'll pay for it.

Quietly and carefully, I did exactly what Awish wrote. I looked into Uncle Skunk's very sad eyes and prayed that I didn't scare the stink out of him.

"You're in excellent hands, Uncle Skunk. Dr. Awish will have you all fixed up soon and back to your family." I closed his cage and snapped the lock shut like a ninja - - a really quiet one.

I went back around the clinic and checked that all the cages were locked, and made sure that the patients were fed and watered before leaving. As I stepped outside the greenhouse, I looked back and realized that each patient had some sort of mouth-related injury.

"You guys are pretty lucky that Awish found you." I closed the door and made a mad dash to the sliding glass doors.

Friday

"COME ON KIDDO, LET'S get you home," Dad tapped me on the shoulder. "I'm sure you're dying to see the guys."

"Thanks again for having him, Crystal. I hope we didn't ruin any of your plans by coming home early. We needed to get ahead of the snow storm coming our way," Dad explained as we walked toward the condo door.

"Well, Todd, I hope you've enjoyed our four days and a half days together. Let's make a date soon, because I think you're going to be missed around here." Aunt Crystal pointed to the trio blubbering away on top of the tissue box.

"Oh Crystal, you have a bee problem. I'll take care of that for you." Dad grabbed a newspaper from the bookshelf and started swinging.

"No, no, no!" I grabbed his arm and stopped the ambush. "The bees are our friends, right Aunt Crystal?"

"Yes, they are *our* friends," she smiled and nodded to my dad. "By the way, Todd, Norman wanted you to know that he has handed out your list of adverbs to all the condo owners. He says you were right; if everyone did their part in powering up The General with a balanced amount of each type of adverb, then the elevator won't need to be replaced. He appreciated all the work that you did on that list."

I hugged Aunt Crystal extra long and choked out a thank you, but I didn't want to leave. I was going to miss all of them, even Buzz. But most of all, I wanted to see Awish. She wasn't home from the hospital yet, and I hadn't heard from her.

Dad lifted my duffel bag and stepped out into the hall.

"Bye, Todd," Honey brushed her eyelashes against my cheek. "I'll miss you. Can you bring some baklava the next time you come? I hope that's soon."

Frizz dove into the hood of my jacket. "Don't tell anyone I'm in here," he muffled, "and I'll just go home with you."

"You silly bee." I reached back into my hood and scooped him out. "Who would take care of Honey and Buzz if you went home with me?" I placed Frizz onto the bookshelf softly and noticed Buzz sitting on top of *Gotta Go, Buffalo*. That was my favorite book when I was younger. I smiled and remembered when Aunt Crystal used to read it to me. But then it occurred to me that Buzz was actually telling me to get lost.

"You're going to miss me, you know." I pointed at Buzz and headed out the door.

"Miss Crystal," Aristotle announced, "You have a voice mail message from Silver Creek Nursery, advising that your banana-apple cider is ready for pick up."

"Oh, I must remember to pick up all the umbrellas I loaned Mr. Peeling at Silver Creek Nursery when I go to pick up my order. My brolly stand is empty." She nodded toward the empty umbrella holder right underneath Sherlock. Aunt Crystal smirked in my direction and then scampered off to listen to her voice mail as she closed the door.

Dad shrugged and we headed toward The General.

*   *   *   *   *

Monday

AFTER FIRST RECESS, MY teacher, Miss McCready, settled our class down in to our desks. "We have unexpected visitors today, but first, I wanted to mention that we are especially glad to have Awish back with us."

I whipped my head around to see Awish coming through the back door with Mrs. Patel. Her nani helped her with her coat, carried her books to her desk, and then kissed her on the top of her head before leaving. Awish looked tired and bruised. I smiled. She smiled back with her eyes. Her mouth was still bandaged from the surgery.

"Awish," Miss McCready continued, "had mouth surgery last week and most likely will need some help this week with her books and some of her school work. I have put together a list of students to be her helper each day, but Chloe, who was to be her first helper, is home sick today."

I shot up my hand like cash was dropping from the sky. "I'll be her helper today." I jumped out of my desk, grabbed a chair, and plopped down beside Awish before Miss McCready could answer.

"Well, I guess that solved that." Miss McCready's eyebrows spiked with surprise.

Deshaun, Eric, and Chad looked at each other as if I had volunteered to count a dump truck load of marbles.

There was a knock at the back door of the classroom, and in walked Curt, grinning from ear to ear. Right behind him was a short man with a gigantic gray mustache that curled like a rollercoaster! His big, white chef's hat had 'Bruno' stitched on the front, making him look like the proudest cook ever. He wore super baggy white pants and a giant white apron that shouted, 'Totally Tasty Pizza!'

Awish and I looked wide-eyed at each other. "Did you enter?" she whispered as well as she could, but then she winced and pointed to her bandages.

I thought her stitches might be pulling.

"Yes, but maybe it was you," I whispered back.

Awish just shook her head *no* this time because it hurt too much to talk. Then she scribbled on a pad of paper;

I wasn't feeling well enough to finish it.

Curt stepped in front of Miss McCready's desk, introduced Bruno, who bowed as if he had just finished playing a piano concert. He announced that one student from Brevda's third grade class had won the Pizza-for-a-Year contest.

The class pounded on their desks with a drum roll. Brrrrrrrr. . . rrrrrrrrr.

"Annnnnnnnnd the winner of the Totally Tasty Pizza Spring Break story is Todd!" Curt pointed to the back of the room where I softly high-fived Awish.

Clapping, cheering, full on fingers-in-the-mouth whistling, and Pizza-Pizza-Pizza chanting filled the classroom! Miss McCready stood with her hands over her ears, but with a huge smile across her face.

The applause continued while my classmates pushed me up to the front of the class so a newspaper reporter could take my picture with Bruno and Curt. I could barely lift the trophy. It was so big!

Then Bruno rolled in the first order. "A number sixteen, stuffed crust, drizzled with honey!"

*   *   *   *   *

Later that evening, they published the newspaper . . .

I Almost Blew my Spring Break

by Todd ~ a third grader at Brevda Heights School

I wanted to stay home. I just wanted to play with my friends.

I wanted to sleep in my own house. And I just wanted to play hockey.

But I didn't get my way. So I was mad at the world. And grumpy with my aunt. And I moped around like I was going to miss out on the best Spring Break ever.

But if I had my way, then I would have missed out.

Because this week I stayed in a condo right out of a sci-fi movie. It had an automated butler named Aristotle, and a TV the size of a wall. I saw and touched cars that were worth huge, big bucks. I traveled in an elevator from history. I made friends with pet bees and watched a helicopter land right in front of my nose. And I met the owner of the Seattle Sting.

But most of all, I met a friend who was much nicer to me than I was to her. Who helped me to solve the riddle of an elevator completely powered by adverbs. Who helped me to see who she was behind her scars. Who trusted me with a secret world where she helps those who hurt just like she did.

She helped me to see things differently.

My wish for everyone is to look for something new to discover, somewhere new to see, and someone new to befriend.

My wish is an Awish for everyone.